PROJECT
MANAGEMENT

ANDY BRUCE
& KEN LANGDON

A Dorling Kindersley Book

LONDON, NEW YORK, MUNICH,
MELBOURNE, DELHI

Senior Editor Adèle Hayward
Senior Designer Caroline Marklew
DTP Designer Jason Little
Production Controller Heather Hughes
US Editor Gary Werner

Senior Managing Editor Stephanie Jackson
Managing Art Editor Nigel Duffield

Produced for Dorling Kindersley
by Cooling Brown
9-11 High Street, Hampton, Middlesex TW12 2SA

Designer Arthur Brown
Editor Amanda Lebentz

Published in the United States by
DK Publishing, Inc.
375 Hudson St.
New York, New York 10014

First American Edition, 2000

10

A catalog record is available from the Library of
Congress

ISBN 0–7894–5971–X

Reproduced by Colourscan, Singapore
Printed in China by WKT

See our complete catalog at
www.dk.com

CONTENTS

4 INTRODUCTION

UNDERSTANDING THE BASICS

6 DEFINING PROJECTS

8 EXAMINING KEY ROLES

10 IDENTIFYING THE ESSENTIALS FOR SUCCESS

12 DEFINING THE STAGES

14 CHECKING FEASIBILITY

16 PRIORITIZING PROJECTS

PLANNING A PROJECT

18 DEFINING THE VISION

20 SETTING OBJECTIVES

22 ASSESSING CONSTRAINTS

24 LISTING
ACTIVITIES

28 COMMITTING
RESOURCES

32 ORDERING
ACTIVITIES

34 AGREEING
DATES

36 VALIDATING
THE PLAN

IMPLEMENTING
A PLAN

38 EXAMINING
YOUR ROLE

40 BUILDING
A TEAM

42 STARTING
POSITIVELY

44 LEADING
EFFECTIVELY

48 DEVELOPING
TEAMWORK

50 MAKING TEAM
DECISIONS

52 MANAGING
INFORMATION

54 COMMUNICATING
CLEARLY

MONITORING
PERFORMANCE

56 TRACKING
PROGESS

58 HOLDING REVIEW
MEETINGS

60 OVERCOMING
PROBLEMS

62 DEALING
WITH CHANGE

64 MAXIMIZING
IMPACT

66 ASSESSING YOUR PROJECT
MANAGEMENT SKILLS

70 INDEX

72 ACKNOWLEDGMENTS

INTRODUCTION

To be successful in today's competitive business world, managers must deliver results on time and within budget. By applying the processes, tools, and techniques shown in Project Management you will maximize performance and ensure optimum results every time. Suitable for managers at all levels, this book equips you with the know-how you need to lead any project, large or small, to a successful conclusion. From starting a project effectively to motivating a team and overcoming problems; every aspect of professional project management is clearly explained. There is a step-by-step guide to project planning, while 101 tips offer further practical advice. Finally, a self-assessment exercise allows you to evaluate your ability as a project manager, helping you to improve your skills, and your prospects for the future.

UNDERSTANDING THE BASICS

Project management provides structure, focus, flexibility, and control in the pursuit of results. Understand what running a project entails and how to improve the likelihood of success.

DEFINING PROJECTS

A project is a series of activities designed to achieve a specific outcome within a set budget and time frame. Learn how to distinguish projects from everyday work and adopt the discipline of project management more widely to improve performance.

1 Greet a new project as an opportunity to develop your skills.

2 Review your work to determine which tasks would be better tackled as projects.

WHAT IS A PROJECT?

A project has clear start and end points, a defined set of objectives, and a sequence of activities in between. The activities need not be complex: painting the staff restaurant is as valid a project as building a bridge. You may be involved in a project without realizing it – for example, if you work in a special team, perhaps outside the normal business schedule, to a deadline. Routine work, on the other hand, is usually ongoing, repetitive, and process-oriented. Some everyday work may lend itself to being managed as a project – tackling it as such will greatly increase your efficiency.

QUESTIONS TO ASK YOURSELF

Q What projects am I involved in at the moment?

Q Has my organization been trying to make changes that might be more likely to happen if tackled as a project?

Q Would I work more effectively if I regarded certain tasks as part of a project?

Q Could project management techniques help to make me more efficient?

WHY USE PROJECT MANAGEMENT?

In today's competitive business environment, a flexible and responsive approach to changing customer requirements is essential. Project management enables you to focus on priorities, track performance, overcome difficulties, and adapt to change. It gives you more control and provides proven tools and techniques to help you lead teams to reach objectives on time and within budget. Organizing activities into a project may be time-consuming initially, but in the long term it will save time, effort, and reduce the risk of failure.

IDENTIFYING THE KEY FEATURES OF PROJECTS

FEATURES	POINTS TO NOTE
DEFINED START AND END All projects have start-up and closure stages.	● Some projects are repeated often, but they are not processes because they have clear start and end points. ● Routine work can be distinguished from projects because it is recurring, and there is no clear end to the process.
ORGANIZED PLAN A planned, methodical approach is used to meet project objectives.	● Good planning ensures a project is completed on time and within budget; having delivered the expected results. ● An effective plan provides a template that guides the project and details the work that needs to be done.
SEPARATE RESOURCES Projects are allocated time, people, and money on their own merits.	● Some projects operate outside the normal routine of business life, others within it – but they all require separate resources. ● Working within agreed resources is vital to success.
TEAMWORK Projects usually require a team of people to get the job done.	● Project teams take responsibility for and gain satisfaction from their own objectives, while contributing to the success of the organization as a whole. ● Projects offer new challenges and experiences for staff.
ESTABLISHED GOALS Projects bring results in terms of quality and/or performance.	● A project often results in a new way of working, or creates something that did not previously exist. ● Objectives must be identified for all those involved in the project.

EXAMINING KEY ROLES

Projects can involve a wide range of people with very different skills and backgrounds. However, there are several pivotal roles common to all projects, and it is important to understand the parts that each of these key people play.

3 Draw up a list of all the people who might be able to help you.

CULTURAL DIFFERENCES

North American projects need a senior sponsor to get off the ground and be accepted by stakeholders. Australia's flatter management structure means that projects also depend on senior support. In the UK, the sponsor can be at a lower level, provided that there is a strong business case for the project.

UNDERSTANDING ROLES

As project manager, you are in charge of the entire project. But you cannot succeed alone, and establishing good relations with other key players is vital. Important project people include the sponsor, who may also be your superior, and who provides backing (either financial or moral); key team members, who are responsible for the overall success of the project; part-time or less senior members, who nevertheless contribute to the plan, and experts or advisers with important roles. There will also be stakeholders, or people with an interest in the project, such as customers, suppliers, or executives in other parts of your organization.

INVOLVING STAKEHOLDERS

Aim to involve your stakeholders at an early stage. Not all stakeholders will be equally important, so identify those who could have a significant effect on the project; and when you draw up the project plan later, consider how regularly they should be consulted. When stakeholders are enthusiastic and strongly supportive of the project, seek their assistance in motivating others. Make sure that you forge strong alliances with those stakeholders who control the resources. Finally, check that everyone understands the reason for their involvement in the project and what its impact on them will be.

4 Build up a good rapport with your main stakeholders.

5 Make sure that your core team consists of people you really trust.

IDENTIFYING KEY PLAYERS AND THEIR ROLES

KEY PLAYER	ROLES

SPONSOR
Initiates a project, adds to the team's authority, and is the most senior team member.

- Ensures that the project is of real relevance to the organization.
- Helps in setting objectives and constraints.
- Acts as an inspirational figurehead.
- May provide resources.

PROJECT MANAGER
Responsible for achieving the project's overall objectives and leading the project team.

- Produces a detailed plan of action.
- Motivates and develops project team.
- Communicates project information to stakeholders and other interested parties.
- Monitors progress to keep project on track.

STAKEHOLDER
Any other party who is interested in, or affected by, the outcome of the project.

- Contributes to various stages of the planning process by providing feedback.
- Might only be involved from time to time.
- May not be a stakeholder for the entire project if his or her contribution is complete.

KEY TEAM MEMBER
Assists the project manager and provides the breadth of knowledge needed.

- Makes a major contribution in examining feasibility and planning a project.
- Lends technical expertise when needed.
- Is directly responsible for project being completed on time and within budget.

TEAM MEMBER
Full or part-time person who has actions to carry out in the project plan.

- Takes responsibility for completing activities as set out in the project plan.
- Fulfills a specialized role if involved as a consultant, or as an individual who is only needed for part of the project.

CUSTOMER
Internal or external person who benefits from changes brought about by the project.

- Strongly influences the objectives of the project and how its success is measured.
- Dictates how and when some activities are carried out.
- Provides direction for the project manager.

SUPPLIER
Provider of materials, products, or services needed to carry out the project.

- Can become very involved with, and supportive of, the project.
- Delivers supplies on time and provides services or goods at a fixed cost, agreed with the project manager at the outset.

IDENTIFYING THE ESSENTIALS FOR SUCCESS

To achieve the desired outcome, a project must have defined and approved goals, a committed team, and a viable plan of action that can be altered to accommodate change. Abide by these essentials to keep you on course for success.

6 Make sure that people understand what you are aiming to achieve.

7 Ask colleagues to read your goals. If any comments are negative, revise the goals.

HAVING CLEAR GOALS

To be successful, a project must have clearly defined goals. These goals must be agreed by all involved, so that everyone proceeds with same expectations. The scope of the project must remain consistent so that it achieves what it set out to accomplish. Whoever agreed to the initiation of the project, usually the project sponsor or customer, should not need to make significant changes to its scope or extent. People who are key to the success of the project must commit their time to it, even if their involvement is only on a part-time basis.

GAINING COMMITMENT

An eager, skilled, and committed team is vital to the success of any project. To this end, the motivational and people management skills of the project manager are paramount. As project manager, it is your responsibility to develop the best team that you can, guide it in the right direction, and ensure that members benefit from the experience. Choose your team carefully and provide training, if necessary. The ongoing support of your superior, sponsor, and other interested parties must also be gained from the outset.

QUESTIONS TO ASK YOURSELF

Q Could I respond to a customer's demand by initiating a project?

Q Whom should I approach to get the project under way?

Q Am I confident that key people will lend their support to make this project successful?

Q Do the overall aims of the project seem achievable?

8 Expect to revise and enhance your project plan at least several times.

PLANNING AND COMMUNICATING

For a project to run smoothly, the resources required must be available at the time you need them. This demands effective front-end planning, taking into account not only people, but also facilities, equipment, and materials. A detailed, complete plan guides the project and is the document that communicates your overall objectives, activities, resource requirements, and schedules. It is also vital that you keep everyone involved fully informed of the plan and update them whenever it changes.

◀ **ACTING EARLY**
Check with your superior that a sufficient budget and realistic time frame have been agreed for the project from the outset. This avoids the success of your project being threatened later because time or money has run out.

BEING FLEXIBLE

In a rapidly changing business environment, the ability to think ahead and anticipate can make the difference between achieving project objectives or not. You must be prepared to change your plans in a flexible and responsive way. It is unlikely that your original plan will be the one you follow all the way, since circumstances and requirements generally change as the project unfolds. This means that you will have to reevaluate the plan regularly and adapt it accordingly. If your project is to succeed, you must be able to anticipate and recognize the need for change, implement it, and measure its impact effectively.

9 Learn to accept the inevitability of change.

10 You can hope for the best, but always plan for the worst.

11

DEFINING THE STAGES

There are five stages to a project: initiation, planning, motivating, monitoring, and closing. Start with a burst, end positively, and recognize the different techniques and skills required to negotiate the three key stages in between.

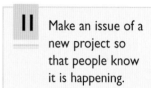

11 Make an issue of a new project so that people know it is happening.

PLANNING A PROJECT

Whether you initiate a project yourself, or your manager or a customer suggests it, the first step in the planning process is to agree a vision for the project, stating exactly what it will achieve. To do this, you will bring together your core team members and people with a close interest in the project's result, known as stakeholders. Having defined a vision, you can identify objectives, agree on actions and resources, order and schedule tasks, and finally validate the plan with all concerned and gain their commitment to it.

IMPLEMENTING THE PLAN

The success of the implementation phase rests with the project team and, ultimately, your ability to lead them. You will have to think about team selection, understand how the team will develop as the project progresses, encourage teamwork, agree on key decisions, and adopt different leadership styles to inspire and motivate different personalities. To gain the commitment of all concerned, make sure that you start with a well-prepared burst, using the authority of your sponsor, manager, and customer to focus everyone on the plan. You must ensure that everyone has access to key project information, and keep communication flowing at all times.

12 Monitor the project consistently from start to finish – problems can occur anywhere along the way.

MONITORING PERFORMANCE

Once the project is under way, you will need to assess how it is faring against objectives and time targets. An efficient monitoring system is vital if you are to deal with problems and changes before they throw a project off-course. During this stage, you will be asking for regular progress reports, organizing team meetings, and identifying milestones that will measure your progress. Once you have identified potential problems and threats, you can then use logical processes to overcome them, and to manage and incorporate changes to the plan when required. Finally, you will gain maximum benefit for your organization by recording your experiences for future reference.

UNDERSTANDING PROJECT DEVELOPMENT

Initiators of project agree a vision

Key people outline project purpose and objectives

Activities and resources are agreed and prioritized

Project plan is approved by all involved

Project manager executes plan, guiding team to achieve goals

Progress is monitored and plan revised as necessary

Project is successfully completed on time and within budget

Project manager greets new colleague with enthusiasm

◀ MAKING AN IMPRESSION

Bring the project team together as early as possible to introduce them, and yourself, informally. It is important to start off on a good footing, so be positive and stress how much you are looking forward to working together as a team.

CHECKING FEASIBILITY

Before starting on a project, you need to be certain that there is a good chance it will be successful. Take the relevant steps to find out whether a project is appropriately timed, feasible, and worthwhile before going ahead with it.

13 Make sure you are not undertaking a task that cannot be achieved.

14 Find out where a project is in danger of failure.

15 Examine whether a given schedule is realistic.

TIMING IT RIGHT

However promising and desirable a project may seem, always carefully examine whether it is the right time to initiate it. Take into account other projects that have already started. Some organizations have so many projects in place that it is not possible for them all to succeed, so you may have to consider postponing the new project or curtailing those that are unlikely to produce valuable results. Since all projects require access to limited or even scarce resources, it is vital that each has a clear reason for existing and that now is definitely the right time for it to happen.

IDENTIFYING DRIVING RESOURCES

Every project is driven by the needs of the organization. The stronger these driving forces, the more likely the project is to succeed. If, for example, a project involves winning back lost customers, the driving force is very strong. To create a list of driving forces, or reasons why your project should go ahead, decide which business concerns the project will have an impact on, and then compare your project with other projects. For example, if there is a driving force behind two projects to increase sales, then the one that, say, doubles sales is more likely to succeed.

QUESTIONS TO ASK YOURSELF

Q Are there any ongoing projects with a higher priority than my own that are taking up key resources?

Q Are my project goals in line with the long-term objectives of my organization?

Q How will the outcome of the project affect the performance of the organization?

Q Could this project damage the chances of another project being successful?

IDENTIFYING RESISTING FORCES

There are always reasons why projects may not be completed. Such forces include people's resistance to change, the weight of the current workload, lack of information or resources, or a dearth of people with the necessary skills. Identify these resisting forces early on so that you can overcome them, or change the timing of the project. A strong resisting force emerges in organizations that frequently initiate projects to change the way people carry out their jobs but fail to see the projects through. If people view a project as simply another management initiative, it will take great skill to motivate them to make it happen.

▼ SEEKING EXPERT ADVICE
Ask a key team member with technical expertise to help you identify reasons why your project may not be successful. They may be able to pinpoint flaws that you had not previously considered.

PREDICTING SUCCESS

A useful technique, known as forcefield analysis, will help you to decide whether the driving forces outweigh the resisting forces, and, consequently, whether the project has a good chance of success. By creating such an analysis, you will be able to see at a glance whether the balance is weighted toward success or failure. To assess the relative impact of each force, remember that drivers range from "one," a weak driver, to "five," an essential need. "Minus one" describes a resisting force that is not much of a threat to the success of the project, while "minus five" shows a force that is very strong, and that, unless you can minimize its impact, is likely to hinder you in achieving the desired project results.

▼ USING FORCEFIELD ANALYSIS
Create a simple diagram, such as the example below, to compare driving and resisting forces. List the driving forces against a vertical grid, and give each column a number between one and five. Do the same with the resisting forces but give them a negative measurement.

Resisting forces						Driving forces				
		Lack of budget								
	Current workload									
					Loss of revenue					
					Current staff frustration					

-5	-4	-3	-2	-1	0	1	2	3	4	5
Strong					Weak					Strong

PRIORITIZING PROJECTS

When managing several projects, you must evaluate which is the most important to your organization in order to allocate time and resources. Seek advice from key people and use the discipline of a master schedule to prioritize effectively.

16 Put your projects in order now and avoid damaging conflicts later.

17 Check that project and organizational priorities align.

CONSIDERING VALUE

Before starting a new project, consider how many people and what resources it needs to meet its objectives. Your aim is to deploy the organization's resources to projects that offer the greatest value in their results. Discuss with your superior, and/or the project initiator, the relative importance of your project. You may wish to hold meetings with your customer or other project team members. The more complex the project, the more important it is to seek the opinion of others before you prioritize.

SETTING PRIORITIES ▼

In this example, the project manager is assigned several projects by her superior. By prioritizing effectively, she is able to complete all the projects successfully. A failure to prioritize, however, leads to disorganization, resulting in none of the projects achieving their intended value.

Project manager reviews projects but cannot decide which is most important

Project manager takes responsibility for three new projects

SCHEDULING PROJECTS

To help you decide early on how best to tackle a string of projects, create a form known as a master schedule. You need not identify all the resources in detail at this stage but write down an estimate. This will enable you to see where there are potential resource clashes between projects and confirm or deny the feasibility of a new project. If, for example, two projects require a crane at the same time, and you only have one available, you must reschedule one project to ensure that the crane is available for both.

Master Schedule

	JAN	FEB	MAR	APR	MAY	JUNE	JULY
Project 1							
Project 2							
Project 3							
RESOURCES							
Project manager	1	2	2	3	2	2	1
Engineers	2	4	4	5	4	1	0
Installation staff	0	3	3	4	2	2	1
Computers	3	5	5	7	4	3	2
Low loader	0	1	2	2	0	0	0
Heavy crane	0	0	1	2	0	0	0

▲ **CREATING A MASTER SCHEDULE**
Create a series of monthly (or, for complex projects, weekly) columns running to the right of the form. List all your ongoing projects and, underneath, detail the resources (people, equipment, materials) you think you are likely to need.

Project manager seeks superior's opinion on which projects should take priority

Project manager completes all three projects successfully

Project manager falls behind with projects because she has failed to prioritize

THINGS TO DO

1. Decide which projects offer the greatest potential value to your organization.
2. If in doubt, seek advice from a superior or the project initiator.
3. Create a master schedule to outline the resources each project requires.
4. If available resources are in conflict, rethink priorities.

PLANNING A PROJECT

An effective plan maps out your project from start to finish, detailing what needs to be done, when, and how much it will cost. Prepare your plan well, and it will guide you to success.

DEFINING THE VISION

Having a clear idea of what a project will achieve is essential if you are to ensure that it will accomplish something of perceived value. With your key team members and sponsor, produce an overall statement that describes the project vision.

18 Be as ambitious as you can, but avoid committing to the impossible.

19 Create a precise vision to avoid ambiguous results.

20 See if others agree with your vision of the future.

DEFINING DESIRABLE CHANGE

Ensure that everyone knows exactly what a project is expected to attain by summarizing its aims. With your key team members and sponsor, create a statement that describes the project vision. For the statement to explain your proposal properly, it must answer the question, "what are we going to change and how?" Check the vision statement with your customers, who may help to refine it by describing what they would expect from such a project. If the project creates something of value for the customer, that is a good indicator of its desirability.

EXAMINING THE IDEAL

To help you outline your vision, try to define what would be ideal. Start from a blank sheet of paper and ask the team to describe what, in an ideal world, the project would change. Avoid being held back by the situation as it is now. While you must remain realistic, you must also be creative in your thinking. Do not allow the way in which you have always done things to deter you from coming up with alternatives. If you involve the customer in this process, avoid giving them the impression that this is how the world will be, but how you would like it to be. Check how feasible the ideal is to arrive at your vision.

CREATING A PROJECT VISION

> Identify a need for change

> Meet with key team members and sponsor

> Define what the project would ideally change

> Assess the likelihood of attaining ideal vision

> Produce a feasible vision statement

DO'S AND DON'TS

✔ Do compromise on the ideal if that is what it takes to arrive at the vision.

✔ Do make the vision statement explain why the project is needed.

✘ Don't ignore obstacles at this stage – they may prove to be major stumbling blocks.

✘ Don't involve too many people this early in the process.

AGREEING A VISION ▶
Encourage team members to question every aspect of the vision to check that it is truly workable and achievable. Make sure that everyone agrees on the way ahead, so that they are committed to attaining the vision.

21 Check at this stage that the vision is clearly worth attaining.

SETTING OBJECTIVES

*O*nce you have agreed on the project
*vision, you must set objectives that will
measure the progress and ultimate success of
the project. Expand the vision to clarify the
purpose of the project, list the objectives,
and then set priorities and interim targets.*

22 Gain agreement on objectives from everyone involved in the project.

23 Make sure that your objectives are measurable.

24 Think how relevant an objective will be when it is achieved.

DEFINING PURPOSE

Expand the vision statement to explain what you
are going to do, how long it will take, and how
much it will cost. Your statement of purpose
should reflect the relative importance of time, cost,
and performance. For example, if you aim to create
a product that competes with the newest solutions
available, the key purpose is performance. Time
frame is the key driver if you must install a new
system before starting international operations.
Cost is the key purpose if you cannot, under any
circumstances, spend more than last year's budget.

DEFINING OBJECTIVES AND INDICATORS

List the specific objectives you wish to achieve,
covering the areas of change that the project
involves. Avoid listing an activity, such as
"complete a pilot," instead of an objective, which
would be to "demonstrate that the project will
achieve the planned business impact." Ensure that
progress against objectives is measurable by
setting an "indicator" against each one. For
example, if your objective is to increase sales of a
new drink, use the indicator of sales volume to
measure success. If you are having difficulty in
arriving at the indicator, ask the question, "How
will we know if we have achieved this objective?"

▼ RESEARCHING STANDARDS

*Nominate a team member to read up on
industry standards. These will provide a
benchmark for your own indicators and a
check on your competitiveness.*

*Team member
studies competitors'
brochures*

SETTING PRIORITIES AND TARGETS

It is unlikely that all the objectives will be equally important to your organization. Give each a priority of one to ten, where one is least important. It will probably be obvious which objectives are significant and which are not, but priorities of those falling in between will be less clear. Discuss and agree these with the team. Then set targets. These may be simple, such as increasing sales by 50 percent, or they may be more complex. If, for example, your objective is to improve customer satisfaction, and the indicator is based on complaints, you must count the number of complaints you now receive, and set a target for reducing them.

POINTS TO REMEMBER

- Objectives should be always be appropriate for the whole organization, not just your own area or department.
- It will be easier to identify targets if you discuss them with others, including your customers.
- Well-defined and appropriate targets will enthuse and motivate team members, encouraging good team morale.

25 Be prepared to drop any objective that has a low priority.

▼ DECIDING ON PROJECT EMPHASIS

Write down your objectives, indicators, priorities, current performance, and targets. This will help you to decide which aspects of the project require most effort and resources.

Key objectives that determine project's success

Priority of objective

Objective	Indicator	P	Current	Target
Improve sales of non-standard products	Increase volume of orders	10	5 million	7.5 million
Improve the speed of decision-making	Reduce time taken to respond to a customer request for a quotation	8	8 weeks	4 weeks
Improve efficiency of preparing customer quotations	(a) Reduce time spent on preparing quotations (b) Cut number of days spent on product training courses	6	(a) 4 days per month (b) 5 days per year	(a) 2 days per month (b) 0 days per year
Improve management accountability for proposals	Make a single manager accountable for producing each customer proposal	6	Not done	In place

Measure of the objective's success

Current level of performance

Desired level of performance

ASSESSING CONSTRAINTS

Every project faces constraints, such as limits on time or money. Occasionally, such constraints may even render the project unfeasible. Make sure that team members understand the constraints in advance, and that they are able to work within them.

26 You can overcome most constraints by planning how to get around them.

▼ LIMITING CHANGE
Talk through any changes you wish to make with your superior, but be prepared to accept that some will not be approved. There may be valid reasons for keeping certain processes or practises intact.

PROTECTING WHAT WORKS

There is little point in change for the sake of it if you can work within the constraints of what currently exists. Even if you identify an area for improvement, it may be better to include the change in a later project, rather than deal with it immediately. This is because too many changes can put a project at risk as people try to cope with too fluid an environment. Also, by taking on too many changes, there is the danger that you will not be able to identify those that have resulted in the success of the project, or indeed, its failure.

ASSESSING TIME CONSTRAINTS

A fast-moving business environment often gives projects a specific window of opportunity. If you are facing a competitor who is to deliver a new product into the stores for the fall season, you must work within that time constraint. You will not benefit from working hard to deliver a competitive product if you cannot launch the new line in time for your customers to place orders. Whether you like it or not, the time constraint has been set and you must work within that boundary.

27 Face up to constraints in a logical fashion.

28 Do your best to find short cuts to success.

EXAMINING RESOURCE LIMITATIONS

Most organizations work within limited resources and budgets, and projects are subject to similar constraints. A new project may entail an extravagant use of resources, so you will need to make sure that they really would be available. But if the success of your project depends on a level of resources that is unlikely to be forthcoming, think again, and alter the objectives of the project. For example, if you can complete the project with fewer resources, then you should make that your plan. Alternatively, if you are in a position to negotiate for more time and money to enable the project to go ahead, do so.

THINGS TO DO

1. Assess whether time is of the essence.
2. Analyze what resources you will need and whether you can afford them.
3. Look into using existing processes or resources.
4. Identify any external constraints, such as legal or environmental regulations.
5. Decide whether to proceed within the given constraints.

29 Explain the constraints to all who agree to take part in the project.

USING EXISTING PROCESSES

In order to reduce project time frames, look at what currently exists. For example, other departments may have plans for change in an associated area that you could capitalize on, product parts that would shortcut design, or current technologies that would avoid the need to invent something new. It is important to consider these issues and reuse as much as possible. It is rarely a good idea to start from scratch, no matter how appealing that may seem.

◀ **CAPITALIZING ON INVESTMENTS**
By studying systems in other departments within your organization, you can capitalize on internal expertise and experience, at the same time saving your organization money.

CASE STUDY

Robert was asked to create a website for his department. Since he did not have the expertise to do this alone, he asked two outside companies that specialized in setting up and maintaining websites to quote for the work.

Robert's sponsor thought that both quotations were too high, and advised Robert to look at the websites already created by other departments within their organization.

Robert particularly liked the site designed and maintained by Anne-Marie, who showed him how to use the software she had bought especially to create her site.

As a result, Robert was able to create the website for his department. In doing so, he not only saved the money that had been allocated specifically for that purpose but also made further use of the software investment originally made by Anne-Marie.

LISTING ACTIVITIES

Having identified your objectives and
constraints, you can now plan in
greater detail. List all the activities needed
to achieve the objectives and divide them
into groups to make it easier to assess what
must be done, when, and by whom.

30 Make sure that
you consult widely
when creating
your activity list.

WHY LIST ACTIVITIES?

Breaking the project work down into smaller units,
or activities, makes it much easier to see how work
overlaps, and how some activities may affect the
timing or outcome of others. Since the list can be
long, it helps to divide activities into groups so that
each set of tasks becomes more manageable and
easier to track when monitoring performance and
progress. Grouping activities also helps you
determine how they fit into a logical sequence for
completion, which aids scheduling and enables you
to assess the number of people and the
skills that will be needed. Listing
activities in this way also reduces the
risk of misunderstandings, since
everyone knows what their tasks are.

*Team member
records each
activity on a
flip chart*

*Team member with
experience of similar
project lends experience
to the brainstorm*

31 Try to describe
each activity
within a short
sentence or two.

DRAWING UP A LIST

Start the process by brainstorming a list of activities. You may need to include more people at this stage. It is often useful, for example, to ask various stakeholders for their views on what it will take to complete the project, especially if it is a complex one. You may also wish to consult other potential team members. Such consultation makes sensible use of other people's expertise and experience. Ideally, if someone in the organization has previously completed a similar project, consult the original project manager and use the previous plan as a checklist. At this stage it is not necessary to concern yourself with the order in which the activities will occur; this comes later.

32 Keep checking your list to see if anything is missing.

PLANNING PROJECT ACTIVITIES

Brainstorm a comprehensive list

Group activities into a logical order

Check that nothing has been missed

Give each group and activity a unique identifying number

Document the activity list

Project manager guides team but does not judge contributions

Team member feels free to suggest an activity

Colleague is aware that this is not the time to pass comment

◀ **BRAINSTORMING ACTIVITIES**
Use a brainstorming session to generate ideas on all the activities needed to complete the project. Note every activity suggested, no matter how inconsequential. Your aim is to draw up a comprehensive list that can be refined later.

GROUPING ACTIVITIES

Break down your long list of activities into smaller, more manageable units by putting the activities into logical groups. You can ask the team to help you or, as project manager, you can do it yourself. Most groups will be obvious. Perhaps certain activities are all concerned with one event occurring later in the project, or some may all involve the same department or people with similar skills. If an activity does not fit into a group, question whether it is really necessary, or leave it as a separate entity.

33 Present your activity list so that it is clear and easy to understand.

GROUPING ACTIVITIES ▶

To group activities effectively, consider the logical order in which they will have to happen. One group, for example, may not be able to start before another is complete. The extract shown lists groups of activities involved in bringing a new product to the manufacturing stage.

ACTIVITIES AND GROUPS

1 **Conduct analysis**
   1.1 Interview customer representatives
   1.2 Consolidate findings into a report
   1.3 Present report to board
2 **Agree product outline**
   2.1 Hold discussions with departments
   2.2 Gain budget approval
3 **Complete design**
   3.1 Take first draft to representative customers
   3.2 Amend to answer customer comments
   3.3 Gain top level agreement to design
4 **Arrange logistics**
   4.1 Order materials
   4.2 Train personnel
   4.3 Engage subcontractors

34 Ask specialists for advice when grouping activities.

35 Put the list away and review it a week later with a fresh perspective.

IDENTIFYING TYPICAL GROUPS

Every project has a start-up phase, or a group of activities that signifies the launch of the project, introduces team members, and records what each person has committed to achieving. Similarly, there should be a group of activities marking the project's closure, involving final checks on performance indicators and finalizing project records for the benefit of subsequent project managers. Finally, most projects need a group of communications activities, for example issuing weekly progress reports or holding a presentation shortly before a planned pilot program goes live.

CHECKING FOR GAPS

Review your list of activities and groups to ensure that it is complete. If you miss this step now and realize later that you have overlooked something, it could have serious implications on the project's budget, schedule, or other resources. Have you identified every activity needed in each group? Go through the planned activities step-by-step: is there anything missing; are you assuming that something will have happened in between activities that you have not actually listed? Once you are confident that each group is complete, give each group and each activity within the group a unique identifying number.

PLANNING A PILOT

Another group of activities that features in many projects, especially when the purpose is to create something entirely new, is a pilot implementation. Typical activities include choosing a limited number of people as a pilot team, implementing the whole project on a limited basis, and keeping records of the experience. By building a pilot phase into the plan, you will have a far less stressful and error-prone time when it comes to rolling out the entire project.

Choose your people for the pilot program carefully and make them aware that they are, for this particular project, guinea pigs. Make sure you communicate your thanks to them after the project, since their agreement to be involved at an early stage probably caused them some problems.

RUNNING A TRIAL ▶
Testing a new idea, even one as complex as an automated production line, allows problems to be solved before a new system is introduced more widely.

COMMITTING RESOURCES

Before starting to implement a project, you must study resource requirements and budgets. The feasibility of the project depends on you and your team being able to justify the expenditure by comparing it favourably with the proposed benefits.

36 Estimate costs carefully – once approved, you are bound by them.

ESTIMATING MANPOWER

Think about who needs to be involved in each activity and for how long in actual worker days. A team member may need to work on a project for a period of 10 days, but if he or she has to work on it for only 30 minutes per day, the total commitment is just five hours. If the member can usefully work on other projects for the rest of the time, the cost to your project will be a fraction of the member's 10-day earnings or charge. But if he or she can make no contribution elsewhere, then your project's budget must bear the full cost.

37 Provide the best supplies, facilities, and equipment you can afford.

CONSIDERING KEY RESOURCES

PEOPLE

| How many people do you need? | Assess who will take on each activity |

| What type of skills do they require? | Identify levels of expertise required |

OTHER RESOURCES

| Are facilities, materials, or supplies essential? | Look at what each activity requires |

| Is information or technology needed? | Examine using existing systems |

MONEY

| What is the total cost of project? | Consider the cost of all the resources |

| Are sufficient funds available? | Check the budget that was agreed |

IDENTIFYING OTHER RESOURCES

While the major cost of a project is generally the people, there are other resources that will have an impact on the budget. For example, you may have to commission market research. Facilities, equipment, and materials may also involve expenditure. Failure to identify all the costs will mean that you lose credibility when others examine the project to balance its costs against its benefits. A comprehensive estimate of costs at this stage also reduces the risk that you will have to request extra funds once the project is up and running.

EXAMINING THE DETAILS

It is not enough to know that the team will need a training room for a month during the project, you will also need to know how large that room needs to be and what kind of equipment you should install in it. The better detail at this stage, the more likely you are to avoid problems during the implementation. This will enable your team to focus on achieving objectives rather than on fixing matters that were poorly planned.

38 Ensure that the budget will allow you to complete all your activities.

CHOOSING A COSTING METHOD

Whatever resources you consider, you can calculate their cost in one of two ways: absolute costing or marginal costing. Absolute costing means calculating the exact cost of the resource. If, for example, a new computer is essential for the project, the amount you pay for it becomes a project cost. If you can use an existing computer, allocate a proportion of its cost to the project. Marginal costing means that you only allocate costs to the project if they would not be incurred if the project did not take place. For example, if an existing computer, which is not being used, is required, the marginal, or extra cost, of the computer is nil. The cost of the computer should not be in the project budget. With practice, marginal costing is easy to calculate and is generally a more accurate measure of the cost of a project to an organization.

MAKING COMPROMISES

In an ideal world, you would gain approval for all the resources you need. In reality, you will probably have to cope with less. The person you most want for a certain task may be unavailable, or the best premises for the project occupied, and you will have to make compromises. Look for compromises that will not threaten the overall aims and objectives of the project. For example, you may be able to recruit a highly skilled worker part-time and allocate the remainder of the work to a less experienced, yet able, team member.

39 Avoid cutting back on tools that the team really need.

40 If resources are scarce, consider your alternatives.

41 Refine a resource plan until anyone could work from it.

DOCUMENTING RESOURCES

The key to ensuring that the resources you require will be available when you need them is to produce a document that all the stakeholders can agree to. This is known as a commitment matrix, because it can be used to remind people of their commitments. Check that the matrix is complete and that every group of activities is comprehensive so that you can be sure that you have identified all the necessary resources.

**CREATING A ▼
COMMITMENT MATRIX**
When you have identified all the resources and estimated costs, document these on a commitment matrix and seek your stakeholders' agreement to it.

Activity as identified by number on activity list

Team members assigned to carry out activity

Resources required to carry out activity

Total cost involved

Activity	People			Resources			Cost
	Who responsible	Who involved	Training needs	Facilities	Equipment	Materials	
2.1	AJB (2 days)	RHC (5 days)	Interview techniques (1 day)	Meeting room Syndicate rooms (2)	OHP (1) Chart (1) Computer (1 day)	Market research report	$23,500

USING OUTSIDE RESOURCES

While many resources will come from within your team or organization, you will need to go outside for others. Make sure that you get competitive quotes from potential suppliers and reach an agreement on costs and performance that makes it easy for both parties to monitor progress tightly. You may need to brush up on your negotiating skills beforehand to ensure that you can win the best deal. While it may seem unnecessary to go into such detail at the outset, the tighter the agreement, the more likely you are to avoid conflict.

MAKING CONTACTS ▶
Ensure that you meet with several potential suppliers and keep their details on record. Even if you decide not to use them this time, an extensive network of contacts could well prove useful for future projects.

GETTING SIGN-OFF

Before you can obtain the official go-ahead for a new project, it must be proven that it is still a business priority and that its benefits to the organization considerably outweigh its costs. This is known as investment appraisal, or cost-benefit analysis, and it is a discipline used widely in many organizations which often have formal systems for the process. If the costs are the same or more than the benefits, the sponsors have three alternatives: they can proceed with the project regardless (although this is seldom desirable unless the strategic value of the project is very important to the long-term aims of the organization); they can modify the objectives and change the activities in a way that reduces costs; or they can cancel the project because it is considered unfeasible.

POINTS TO REMEMBER

● If your organization has an official system for obtaining sign-off for a project, this should be followed.

● Finance departments can provide useful feedback on your estimates by comparing your project's costs with others.

● The benefits of a project should never be exaggerated – promises will be expected to be delivered.

42 Be prepared to justify your choices, dates, and budgets.

ORDERING ACTIVITIES

Not all activities can, or need, to start at the same time to meet the project's planned completion date. Put activities into a logical sequence, estimate the duration of each, and then use clear documentation to help you devise a project schedule.

43 Remember that activities can be carried out in parallel.

44 Ask whoever is responsible for an activity to give you their estimated start and end dates.

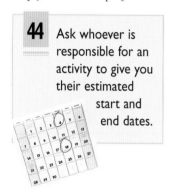

CONSIDERING ORDER

Having completed a list of the activities required to complete the project, look at how they interrelate. Decide which activities should start immediately or first, which need to be completed before moving on to the next, and work through all the activities until the end of the project. Some activities will be the culmination of a number of others. For example, the team will probably need to complete several activities before it can make a presentation to the people involved in a pilot program. Important activities will be review meetings.

ESTIMATING ACTIVITY TIMES

To draw up an effective schedule, you need to know how much time each activity is likely to take. It is important to estimate these durations accurately, since poor guesswork may throw the entire project off course. Team members should also have input to ensure that they agree with the estimated activity times and will be able to work to the schedule that you produce. If there is major doubt as to how long an activity could take, estimate best and worst case scenarios and work out a compromise between the two. If a project is under time pressure this will help to identify where you could reduce the overall time frame.

QUESTIONS TO ASK YOURSELF

Q Do I have time to do a trial run of an activity to test how long it might take?

Q Could I estimate the duration of an activity more reliably if I sought expert advice?

Q Have I looked at previous project plans to see how long similar activities took?

Q Could I ask other project managers for their advice?

Q Am I confident that my estimates are realistic?

45 Get expert help to draw the first network diagram.

WORKING WITH A NETWORK DIAGRAM

A network diagram shows the relationship between activities, and which ones depend on the completion of others. The diagram may be simple or highly complex, according to how many activities there are and how they interrelate. Where there are several routes through a network, there is a chance to complete tasks simultaneously. Indicate the duration of each task and add up the total time required to complete each route to find the longest route through the network. This longest route is known as the critical path, which shows the shortest possible duration for the project.

Key

▬▬ *Critical path (minimum duration 19 days)*

➤ *Noncritical path (minimum duration 6 days)*

◯ *Activities that can be undertaken simultaneously*

◯ *Activity that can only start once previous activities are complete*

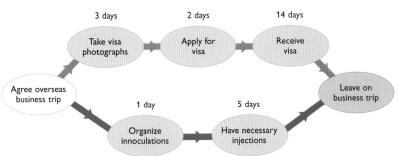

LOOKING FOR SLACK

You can also use the the network diagram to find opportunities for shortening the project schedule. This involves looking at where you can cut the amount of time it takes to complete activities on the critical path, for example, by increasing the resources available to that activity. Take another look at the diagram to identify where any other routes might have some slack. You may then be able to reallocate resources to reduce the pressure on the team members who are responsible for activities on the critical path.

▲ CREATING A NETWORK DIAGRAM
The network above sets out activities to be completed before a business trip. Progress on the critical path must be monitored closely, since a delay in carrying out these activities will affect the project end date.

46 Keep to the critical path to stay on schedule.

AGREEING DATES

Having identified how the activities follow on from one another, and worked out the minimum duration of the project, you can now set real dates. Plot these carefully, taking any potential conflicts into account, and then agree them with the team.

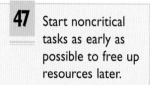

47 Start noncritical tasks as early as possible to free up resources later.

48 Remember to keep your Gantt chart up to date at all times.

USING A GANTT CHART ▼
This Gantt chart lists tasks on the left and the project timeline in weeks across the top. The bars show when tasks start and finish, providing a clear visual overview of project tasks and timings.

CALCULATING DATES

Use the network diagram to help you calculate start and end dates for each activity. Begin with the first activity and work through all the others, starting each as early as possible to allow as much time as you can. If an activity is not on the critical path, start and end dates can be more flexible, since these will not necessarily affect the overall project duration. Finally, plot the dates against a timeline to produce a Gantt chart. These charts are useful for early schedule planning, for showing individual timelines on complex projects, and for comparing progress to the original schedule.

Timeline shows length of project

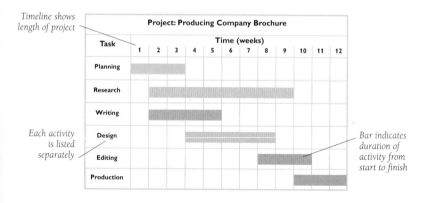

Each activity is listed separately

Bar indicates duration of activity from start to finish

LOOKING FOR OVERLAP

To check that the dates you have calculated are realistic, refer to your Gantt chart, commitment matrix, and master schedule. The Gantt chart shows you immediately where project activities overlap. Where an overlap exists, the commitment matrix will reveal whether an activity requires the same resource at the same time. In these circumstances, you will have to amend that activity's start and finish dates. The final piece of information comes from looking at the master schedule, which will tell you whether there is any overlap in resources between two projects or more.

49 Encourage your team members to be realistic about dates.

GAINING AGREEMENT

Discuss the dates you have set with the key people to make sure that they are truly available at the time they are needed. You may have to hold discussions with their managers if they are being held to other commitments elsewhere in the organization. On long projects, remember to allow for the fact that team members will not necessarily be available every day, even if they are theoretically working full-time on the project. The percentage of time they will be available is often around two-thirds of the calendar year, or 240 days. Use that number to check that you have allowed time off for vacations, sickness and training.

◀ **PLANNING VACATIONS**
Ask team members to book in their vacation time as early as possible in order to avoid last-minute alterations to the schedule. Use a wallchart to show the team's vacation commitments.

VALIDATING THE PLAN

No matter how well you have written your plan, the unexpected is bound to occur and circumstances are certain to change. It is vital to work closely with the team and stakeholders to anticipate and preempt potential problems.

50 Make a point of discussing the final plan with your customers.

51 Use other project managers' experience to identify threats.

IDENTIFYING THREATS

Now that you have a schedule for all the activities needed to complete the project, brainstorm a list of potential threats and analyze each for its impact on your plan. People outside the team can be very helpful in this process, which also encourages the team to defend the plan against constructive criticism, making them more determined to overcome any obstacles. Deal with every threat in turn, paying most attention to those that have an impact on activities on the critical path so that you can work out your best counterattack in advance.

▼ ANTICIPATING PROBLEMS

Bring together a representative group of stakeholders, particularly customers, and those with relevant experience, and ask what could, in their opinion, go wrong.

Customer identifies potential problem

Sponsor weighs up impact on project

Project manager suggests a way of overcoming threat

Team member notes threats and suggested counterattacks

PREEMPTING PROBLEMS

Now get the team to focus on preventing the problems from occurring. The question is, "What can we do to reduce the probability that each potential problem might occur?" If the plan is dependent on the weather, for example, you may change the timing of the work schedule. If key materials are in short supply or there is the possibility of a labor strike in your own organization or that of your supplier, you must consider ways to address these problems early on.

52 If you suspect that someone may be promoted off the team, take steps to train a replacement.

53 Check contingency plans with whoever supplies resources.

54 Table the plan, with contingencies, at a review meeting.

CONTINGENCY PLANNING

It is not possible to preempt every eventuality that could harm the project. Get the team to consider what it will do if certain threats occur, and how to minimize the impact of the threats. If the project needs a new piece of software, for example, look at what you could do if it were to be delivered late. If the software is late, and you need a contingency system, it will probably add to the cost of the project. Bring this to the attention of those in control of budgets. You may then have to revisit your cost-benefit analysis.

COMPLETING THE PLAN

From the list of threats and the discussion on preempting problems and contingency planning, you will be able to decide what changes to make to the plan. Make these alterations and the plan is complete. The team has its "baseline" or starting point. It knows what the situation is now, and what will be the result of implementing the plan. Remember, though, that you must ensure that the team is prepared for the fact that the planning and implementation process is rarely sequential. It is likely they will have to recast some of the plan as activities are carried out and changes occur.

POINTS TO REMEMBER

● The more stakeholders who validate a plan, the more likely it is to be implemented.

● If there is a strong likelihood that a contingency plan will be needed, that course of action should become the actual plan.

● Time spent validating the plan and preparing for problems in advance is rarely wasted.

● The entire plan should be double-checked by the project manager before implementation.

IMPLEMENTING A PLAN

The success of a project plan relies on the people who execute it. Equip yourself with the leadership skills necessary to build a strong, committed team and guide it to the desired outcome.

EXAMINING YOUR ROLE

To successfully implement a project plan, it is important to understand what is involved at the outset. Familiarize yourself with the key tasks, responsibilities, and skills involved, and you will be better prepared to lead a project team successfully.

> **55** Know the project plan inside out and answer questions authoritatively.

> **56** Keep the business priorities in mind, especially when the project goal is to make a profit.

DEFINING YOUR RESPONSIBILITIES

As project manager, you have overall responsibility for the project's success. Having negotiated the planning process, you must now translate the plan into action. This involves selecting the right team members, focusing and motivating them to achieve project goals, and helping them to develop both as individuals and as team workers. The project manager must also build good relationships with stakeholders, run team meetings effectively, administrate and coordinate, and communicate clearly on all levels every step of the way.

TAKING THE LEAD

A successful project manager is both a manager and leader. Leaders command authority and respect, follow up plans with actions, and are able to inspire and motivate others. They also adopt different leadership styles as circumstances dictate. You can develop these skills through training and experience: try practicing outside work by taking office at your local civic club. Mainly, you develop leadership skills by taking responsibility for objectives. You may have to start by becoming accountable for a group of activities before you can take on an entire project.

Is a good communicator

Can manage and adapt to change

Possesses the necessary technical expertise

Puts the customer first

Has team building and negotiating skills

Select final team members and allocate responsibilities

Launch the project successfully

Motivate and focus team on objectives

Organize information systems

Communicate key information

◀ **EVALUATING SKILLS**
To be an effective leader, you must develop several important attributes. This example shows some of the essential qualities of a successful project manager.

QUESTIONS TO ASK YOURSELF

Q Are you willing to stay with the project for its entire term?

Q Are you interested in developing people and helping them to become leaders?

Q Do you have a real interest in working on the project?

Q Can you delegate objectives to the team as well as tasks?

ASSESSING YOURSELF

If you are not sure whether you have what it takes to be a leader, ask someone whose opinion you respect for objective comments. For example, you could talk to people with whom you have worked in the past to ascertain how they regard you. If they plainly feel that they could work for you, then that is a good indicator. Once you have gathered the facts, you can create a picture of where you want to be in the future, and put together a plan for developing the necessary skills.

BUILDING A TEAM

Having planned the project with a core team, now ensure that you have the full complement of people with the right mix of skills and personalities to see it through. Choose your team carefully, bearing in mind the vital team roles that should be covered.

57 Try not to have preconceived ideas about people – judge as you find.

QUESTIONS TO ASK YOURSELF

Q How much do I know about a potential team member and do I trust him or her?

Q Will I be able to work comfortably with him or her?

Q Am I confident that all the team members will get along with one another?

Q Does the team member have the necessary skills and talent to do the job – or will training be required?

ASSESSING AVAILABILITY

Refer back to your commitment matrix to identify the skills and people needed to complete the project. The chart will tell you who is required, for how long, and when. Draw up a list of candidates who might be suitable for each part and find out whether they are available. You may need to negotiate with other managers if you wish to appoint staff working in different areas of the organization. Your own project is almost certainly not the only one in progress, so you may also need to talk to whoever is coordinating the resources deployed on all of the projects.

CHOOSING THE RIGHT PEOPLE

Apart from having the necessary skills, the people you want to attract are those who will come willingly. It is much easier to work with people who are enthusiastic about the project, so it pays to hold discussions with potential team members to find out whether they are eager to work on the project. Think also of the team as a whole. Will each team member fit in with the others? Is there any conflict between potential members? You will, of course, help them to form a team under your leadership, but it is better to start off with people who are sympathetic to each other.

58 Be frank with potential team members – ask if they identify with the project's aims.

59 Build a team that takes advantage of each individual's skills without overburdening their weaknesses.

CONSIDERING ROLES

In any team you will look for people to carry out a team role as well as their functional role. To operate efficiently you, as the team leader, will want someone to perform the roles of critic, implementer, external contact, coordinator, ideas person, team builder, and inspector. Most team members will fit strongly into one or more of these roles. You need them all, and if one is not present, you will have to take the role on yourself. If, for example, you see that no one is challenging the team's standards, quality, and way of working, you are lacking a critic. Keep challenging the team yourself until you see someone else leaning toward this role. Discuss these roles in an open manner, encourage friendly conversations, and you will build one of the most important qualities of a group – team spirit. Remember that only as a team will you be able to achieve the project's objectives.

DO'S AND DON'TS

✔ Do allow people to settle into roles without being pushed.

✔ Do double or treble up on roles when a project team only has a few members.

✔ Do ask a stakeholder to take on a role if it is not being played.

✗ Don't attempt to shoehorn a personality into a particular role.

✗ Don't expect people to continue playing a role if they become uncomfortable in it.

✗ Don't take on a role yourself if it means appearing insincere.

KEY TEAM ROLES

COORDINATOR
Pulls together the work of the team as a whole.

CRITIC
Guardian and analyst of the team's effectiveness.

IDEAS PERSON
Encourages the team's innovative vitality.

IMPLEMENTER
Ensures smooth-running of the team's actions.

EXTERNAL CONTACT
Looks after the team's external contacts.

INSPECTOR
Ensures high standards are maintained.

TEAM BUILDER
Develops the teamworking spirit.

60 Encourage criticism, but ask the critic to supply alternatives, too.

STARTING POSITIVELY

Once you have the right team in place, it is important to launch a new project in a positive manner. Encourage teamwork by inviting everyone to an informal gathering at the outset, and record the project's existence formally to clarify its purpose.

61 Ask the most senior person possible to attend a project launch.

62 Listen to reactions from newcomers and be prepared to review activities.

USING YOUR SPONSOR ▼
The first team meeting offers your sponsor an important platform. Invite him or her to address the team and express belief and commitment in the project. This is invaluable for encouraging team spirit.

STARTING ACTIVELY

At an early stage, gather the team together for a full initiation session to let them know exactly what the project is all about. Explain what the targets and constraints are, let everyone know how the project will benefit them, and establish ground rules relating to the sharing of information and decision-making. Keep the session two-way so that people can ask questions. By the end of the meeting, everyone should understand what needs to be done and feel motivated to achieve it.

Colleague feels valued in his new role

Sponsor greets team with positive enthusiasm

Team member learns of the project's importance

Team member is impressed by sponsor's confidence in the project manager and team

WRITING A START-UP REPORT

A start-up report should make everyone aware of the vision that has inspired the project and the measures of success the team will be aiming for. You may also document the resources allocated to the project, and give some indication of the risks that are involved. Finally, it is a good idea to name all the stakeholders so that everyone knows who they are, and ask key people who are underpinning the project to endorse it by adding their signatures to the document. These will include the project manager and project sponsor.

 63 Keep reports free of jargon and complex language.

 64 Ask for signatures to the plan as a formal agreement.

STRUCTURING A START-UP REPORT

PARTS OF A REPORT	FACTORS TO INCLUDE
VISION An explanation of the overall aim of the project.	● Clarify exactly why the project has been initiated and what it is setting out to achieve. ● Spell out the benefits of the project to the entire project team and to the organization as a whole.
TARGETS A summary of indicators, current performance, and target figures.	● Provide clear information on how the success of the project will be measured. ● Explain what business results are expected to have been achieved by the end of the project.
MILESTONES Special events or achievements that mark progress along the way.	● Summarize milestones to remind everyone of what they will have to deliver at each stage of the project ● Set out your milestones so that they divide the project into logical, measurable segments.
RISKS AND OPPORTUNITIES A list of the potential risks and additional opportunities.	● Explain what needs to be avoided when team members carry out their roles. ● Highlight any areas where improvements could be made in order to gain even greater benefit from the project.
LIST OF STAKEHOLDERS A directory of all the stakeholders involved in the project.	● Name all interested parties and list their credentials to add to the credibility of the project. ● List all your customers, and state what each customer expects to gain from the project.

LEADING EFFECTIVELY

There are many different styles of leadership, but because projects rely on good teamwork, it is important to favor a consensus-building, rather than a dictatorial, approach. To lead a project well, you must be able to motivate your team.

65 Be a manager whom people want to seek out, rather than avoid.

66 Show your enthusiasm for the project, even when under pressure.

UNDERSTANDING STYLES

There is a spectrum of possibilities in leadership styles, and you will need to adopt them all at certain points in the project. While your approach may need to vary from a dictatorial style to a consensus-seeking one, the predominant style you adopt should depend on your organization, the nature of the project, the characteristics of the team, and your own personality.

CHOOSING A LEADERSHIP STYLE

LEADERSHIP STYLE	WHEN TO USE IT
DICTATORIAL Making decisions alone, taking risks, being autocratic and controlling.	This style may be appropriate if the project faces a crisis, and there is no time to consult. However, since it discourages teamwork, it should be used sparingly.
ANALYTICAL Gathering all the facts, observing and analyzing before reaching decisions.	This style, which requires sound analytical skills, may be used when a project is under time pressure or threat, and the right decision must be made quickly.
OPINION-SEEKING Asking for opinions from the team on which to base decisions.	Use this style to build team confidence and show that you value people's views, as well as to impress stakeholders, who like to be consulted.
DEMOCRATIC Encouraging team participation and involvement in decision-making.	This is an essential style to be used on a regular basis to empower team members, and help strengthen their commitment to a project.

CULTURAL DIFFERENCES

Project managers in the UK often create an inner circle of key team members to speed up decision-making, while in the US, the entire team is brought together frequently. In Japan, decisions are reached by consensus, in which unanimous agreement is reached through a laborious process.

CHANGING STYLES

Be prepared to change your leadership style to suit the circumstances and the team, even if you feel uncomfortable for a while because the style you are adopting does not come naturally. For example, some managers find consultation annoying and time-wasting, while other managers are so intent on gaining consensus that decisions take too long, and the project suffers as a result. The key to making good consensus decisions is to listen carefully to everyone before indicating which way they are leaning. A decision is then reached accordingly, unless someone can argue most convincingly that it is the wrong move.

LEADING APPROPRIATELY

Each member of a team has a unique personality and style. Take time to study each individual and understand what motivates them so that you can provide the level of guidance they need. Some team members will prefer to be set objectives, with the project manager delegating responsibility to them for how they should be tackled. Others will react better to being given specific tasks. Use the appropriate style for each individual.

▼ ADOPTING A HANDS-OFF APPROACH
Motivate an experienced, capable team member by allowing them to use their own initiative. Provide support and guidance but avoid interfering too heavily.

◄ BEING HANDS-ON
Explain clearly what you expect from a new or less confident worker, who will need close supervision and encouragement.

Obtaining Results

There are two major factors to consider when deciding which style of leadership to use. If the project is under time pressure, there may be no alternative to the dictatorial style because you do not have the luxury of time to consult. If you want to gain commitment, you must involve others in the key decisions to increase their willingness to make the decision work. Whichever style you choose, the quality of the decision is vital. Before you impose a decision, ensure that you have all the facts to prove that it is the right thing to do.

Points to Remember

- The team should not be expected to do everything your way, provided that their results are satisfactory.
- When a small point is important to a member of the team, it is wise to yield – you should be trying to win the war, not every single battle.
- If, in your view, the success of the project is in any way threatened, that is the time to be assertive.

67 Look for ways to use conflict constructively.

Resolving Conflict

Personality clashes are inevitable when many people work together. There may be differences of opinion or disputes that arise from people having different standards on quality of work, or there may be one or two team members who simply do not get along. If team members disagree, find a way of resolving the conflict either by taking on the role of decision-maker yourself or by using diplomacy in talking to the people concerned.

Conflicts can sometimes arise as a result of schedules. For example, one team member might want more time for a group of activities, which a colleague feels is unnecessary. Work through the schedule with both parties to arrive at a solution that suits everyone.

◄ **BEING A DIPLOMAT**
When a conflict between team members threatens the project's success, you will have to mediate. Look for a solution that brings some source of satisfaction to each party. Such a compromise will allow the project to move on.

CASE STUDY

Sally, a key member of the project team, was responsible for leading a small team of her own. As the project got under way, Tom, the project manager, was surprised to see that Gerald, one of Sally's most competent and confident team members, was contributing very little to team meetings. He took Gerald aside informally and asked how he was getting on. Although Tom was reluctant to criticize Sally,

by listening carefully, Tom realized that Gerald had been used to far more involvement in making decisions on other project teams he had worked for. It was evident that Gerald found Sally too abrupt. Tom approached Sally and asked her to think about her leadership style with Gerald. As a result, she spent more time discussing issues with him, and Gerald went on to play a far more active part in team meetings once again.

◀ **LEADING WISELY**

Sally's abrupt approach and her tendency to make all the decisions was very demotivating for Gerald, who liked to be able to use his initiative. Rather than take matters into his own hands, Tom asked Sally to consider the matter and take any action she deemed appropriate. Sally decided to make a point of involving Gerald more to make him feel valued. As a result, his performance soon began to improve.

STANDING BACK

It can be a hard lesson to learn that a good leader will allow people to make a mistake. You may, from your experience, know that the team is taking a decision that is not in the best interests of the project. But if you take control, you are not necessarily helping them to improve. If they never see the effects of their decisions, they will never learn which ones led to difficulties. Obviously, you must use your discretion as to when to step back. The team's development is important, but not as vital as achieving the objectives of the project.

68 Show your team respect, and they will show it to you.

69 Introduce new ideas to maintain the team's interest.

EXERCISING LEADERSHIP SKILLS

To lead your team effectively, you must:
● Ensure that everyone is working toward agreed, shared objectives;
● Criticize constructively, and praise good work as well as find fault;
● Monitor team members' activities continuously by obtaining effective feedback, such as regular reports;

● Constantly encourage and organize the generation of new ideas within the team, using techniques such as brainstorming;
● Always insist on the highest standards of execution from team members;
● Develop the individual and collective skills of the team, and seek to strengthen them by training and recruitment.

DEVELOPING TEAMWORK

For a team to be successful, people must learn to pull together. Encourage teamwork by promoting a positive atmosphere in which people compete with ideas rather than egos, and recognize the team's changing needs as it progresses through the project.

70 When individuals perform well, praise them in front of the team.

CULTURAL DIFFERENCES

Project managers in the US often use rousing speeches and rhetoric to motivate staff and build team spirit. In the UK, an eloquent speech will also strengthen commitment, but the approach has to be far more subtle. In Japan, managers seek to build strong ties of loyalty by emphasizing the importance of the project to the company.

ENCOURAGING TEAMWORK

Make sure that each member of the team recognizes the value that everyone else is bringing to the project. Encourage them to appreciate one another's skills and capabilities, and to work together to achieve the highest standards. Praise the team as well as individuals so that everyone feels that they are doing a good job. If everyone understands who is playing which role and who has responsibility for what, there should be no reason for conflict and uncertainty. As project manager, you must be seen to be fair to everyone, since showing any favoritism can also lead to dissent. Use project review meetings to strengthen teamwork and help build team confidence.

UNDERSTANDING TEAM DEVELOPMENT

All teams go through a series of stages as they develop, described as forming, storming, norming, and performing. Your aim is to move the team on to the performing stage, where they are working well together, as quickly as possible. With strong leadership, the difficult initial stages of bringing the team together and settling them into the project can be negotiated smoothly. Use your authority to swiftly defuse any conflict and put a stop to any early political maneuvering.

POINTS TO REMEMBER

- Not every team member will be equally committed to the project at the outset.
- It should be expected that everyone will have to go through the storming stage, but this can be creative if managed positively.
- It is important to develop creative team members rather than conformists.
- People need to be comfortable to work well together.

DEALING WITH STAGES IN THE LIFE OF A PROJECT TEAM

FORMING
Members feel tentative and unsure about their project roles

Explain what everyone will contribute

STORMING
Members try to assert their positions and jockey for seniority

Make it clear that teamwork is crucial to success

NORMING
Working practices and processes are agreed and established

Foster team spirit and develop the team's skills

PERFORMING
Team works positively and productively to achieve project goals

Build team confidence in its collective ability

Keep the team focused on completing project

MAINTAINING MOMENTUM

There are two more stages that occur in a team's long-term life, known as "boring" and "mourning." The first applies to a project lasting a long time, where team members may stop looking for new challenges or new and improved ways of doing things. Put in effort at this stage to encourage innovation. Mourning occurs when a team has bonded well and reacts to a member's departure by grieving their loss. Decide how to replace that person and reassure remaining team members that you have every confidence in their ability.

71 Help people to define problems for themselves.

72 Remember that relationships will change over time.

49

MAKING TEAM DECISIONS

W*hen mapping out the future course of the project, quality decision-making is paramount. To ensure that you make the right decisions as a team, establish a logical process that you follow every time. Then use feedback to double-check quality.*

73 Ensure that you know all the facts before making a decision.

POINTS TO REMEMBER

- Using a decision-making process may take time initially, but speed will improve with experience.
- The decision-making process can be clearly explained to sponsors and stakeholders.
- People implement decisions more willingly when they have participated in them.

USING A LOGICAL PROCESS

Following the same process in making every decision has several benefits. The team becomes faster at decision-making, since if everyone knows the process, they quickly eliminate invalid options and come to the most sensible alternative. The quality of decisions improves because using a process removes some of the guesswork and, finally, any team members who might initially have been against a decision are more likely to accept it if it has been reached via a process of consensus.

DEFINING THE IDEAL

The team must agree on the criteria against which they wish to measure a decision and the ideal performance against each criterion. Suppose, for example, you are looking at two options for a supplier of services to the project. Ask team members to brainstorm what an ideal solution would look like. Ask the questions, "What do we want this solution to do for us?", and "What benefits should we look for?" This list then gives the team a way of filtering options and comparing the alternatives.

▼ **AGREEING CRITERIA**
Brainstorm a list of criteria against which you will measure decisions, and ask a team member to record each suggestion on a flipchart so that everyone is using the same wording to describe the ideal.

EVALUATING OPTIONS

With the team's help, identify which criteria are the most important. You may find that three or four stand out as being vital. Now measure all your options against the ideal agreed for each criterion. The process is logical, but good creative thinking is still needed to evaluate the options effectively. Having carried out this evaluation, you may find that the decision is obvious. If not, take the next most important criterion and repeat the exercise. Continue until one option stands out, or until the team is certain that, say, two options have nothing between them. Where that is the case, choose the option you believe will be the most acceptable to your sponsor and other stakeholders.

74 Encourage debate on all the options to gain a wider perspective.

75 Ask an objective critic to look at your decision and give you feedback.

MAKING SAFE DECISIONS

What would be the impact if you made a wrong decision? If it would be catastrophic, you may want to think again and find a less risky route. Finally use the acronym SAFE to validate the choice. SAFE stands for:

- Suitable: is the decision really the most suitable one, given the current state of the project?
- Acceptable: is the decision acceptable to all the stakeholders who have an interest in it?
- Feasible: will it be practical and feasible to implement the solution, given the project's time and resource constraints?

- Enduring: will the solution endure to the end of the project and further into the long term?

Remember that the SAFE test can be applied as a quick and useful check for any decision made by teams or individuals.

VALIDATING DECISIONS ▶
Check that you have made the right decisions by asking your sponsor or other stakeholders, such as customers or suppliers, for their views.

MANAGING INFORMATION

*E*veryone *must have easy access to key project information whenever they need it. You can ensure that all the project data is kept up to date and recorded efficiently by setting up a knowledge center and appointing a coordinator to manage it.*

76 Keep notes of errors made and lessons learned for future reference.

77 Index information clearly to make it more accessible.

78 Check that data is being updated on a regular basis.

ASSESSING INFORMATION

During the life of a project you will produce a wealth of data. Each item of information should be regarded as potentially valuable, either to your own project or to a subsequent one. It will be obvious what must be stored, but try to think more widely. If, for example, a project involves researching a benchmark for productivity, remember that this may be of interest to other parts of the organization. Any work undertaken on risk management, new techniques used, or even the way in which the team has been structured could prove valuable in the future.

ORGANIZING DATA

Project data can be grouped into two types: general planning information, such as the vision statement, objectives, master schedule, and network diagram; and general data, such as any background information that might be needed to carry out activities. It may be a good idea to divide activity information into three further groups: completed activities; activities currently in progress; and activities still to be started. In this way, everyone will know exactly where to look for the information they need. Beware of amassing lots of unnecessary data, however, because this will simply clog up what should be an efficient, easy-to-use system.

THINGS TO DO

1. Explain to the team what type of information is to go into the knowledge center.
2. Ensure that the knowledge coordinator has the necessary software tools to run the center efficiently.
3. Ask the coordinator to remind people of deadlines for completing activities and progress reports.

APPOINTING A COORDINATOR

In projects where the information flow is limited, you will probably be able to manage the data yourself. However, in a large project with a mass of information, it will pay dividends to put a team member in charge of the knowledge center, either full-time or part-time. Such a person is known as the knowledge coordinator, and the most likely candidate for the job is the team member who most takes on the role of coordinator. He or she will keep the planning documentation up to date and collect, index, and make available all the important project information gathered by the team.

CULTURAL DIFFERENCES

Business organizations in North America tend to lead the way when it comes to saving information and making it available to the organization as a whole. Most organizations in the US employ knowledge coordinators at several levels, meaning that project managers are able to access information quickly and easily. Knowledge coordinators are gradually making their presence felt in Europe as their importance becomes recognized.

Team member updates coordinator on progress of an activity

Coordinator records information for knowledge centre

◀ **UPDATING PROJECT INFORMATION**
The knowledge coordinator plays an important role as the administrator of the project plan, collecting progress reports, updating network diagrams, Gantt charts, and activity reports.

COMMUNICATING CLEARLY

The better the communication, the more smoothly a project will flow. Make sure that everyone who needs it has easy access to project information, and that you encourage two-way communication by listening and asking for feedback.

79 Avoid sending any message that could hinder, rather than help, your project.

80 Tell the team what they want and need to know.

81 Meet often with team members on a one-to-one basis.

SHARING KNOWLEDGE

Consider who needs what information, in what format, and when. Refer to the list of stakeholders in the start-up report to ensure that noone is forgotten. Concentrate on people whose access to information will be crucial to the project, but do not ignore others with less significant roles. Plan how you are going to make the information available, bearing in mind that these activities should take up as little time as possible. Your knowledge coordinator must know what the priorities are. For example, if a customer changes requirements, the team needs to know urgently.

USING INFORMATION TECHNOLOGY

Make the most of new technology to improve communications. Email is an extremely useful time-saving device, provided it is handled correctly. The main point to remember is that you receive as many emails as you send, which means that you should think carefully before writing each message. Is it absolutely vital to send a message now? Is it the most effective means of communication for the current situation? As a guideline, send as few emails as possible to do the job well, and you will get the best out of electronic communication. Take care too, with compatibility. Emailing an electronic file to someone who does not have the same software results in an immediate communication breakdown. This wastes time.

ENCOURAGING TWO-WAY COMMUNICATION

The team is the primary conduit for information between the customer, other stakeholders, and you, the project manager. It is important to encourage honest feedback. Use open questions, such as the ones below, to ascertain their real feelings and opinions.

❝ *How do you think we could improve the way we are working on this project?* ❞

❝ *How are our customers reacting to the work we are doing – do they appear to be satisfied?* ❞

❝ *Having completed that activity, is there anything you would change if you had to do it again?* ❞

❝ *Are you aware of any negative reactions concerning the progress of the project?* ❞

LISTENING TO OTHERS

Encourage the project team to be open and honest with you by showing that you value their opinions and are willing to listen to them. Make it clear that even negative feedback is viewed as a positive opportunity for improvement, and ensure that team members are not intimidated by fear of any repercussions when they do express criticisms. Keep your door open for stakeholders, too – it is important that they feel they can approach you with queries or problems. Always listen to people carefully – because only through listening can you determine whether your messages have really been understood.

| 82 | Be interested both in what people say and how they are saying it. |

Team member feels free to voice an honest opinion

Colleague provides both negative and positive feedback

◀ INVITING FEEDBACK
Take team members aside, either individually or in small groups, and solicit feedback by asking for their comments on how they think the project is progressing.

MONITORING PERFORMANCE

Effective monitoring keeps a project on track in terms of performance, time, and cost. Focus on your plan while acting fast to tackle problems and changes in order to stay on course.

TRACKING PROGRESS

Even the best-laid plans can go awry, which is why it is crucial to have an early-warning monitoring system. Make sure that you understand what effective monitoring involves and how to set up a process that will highlight potential problems.

83 Keep comparing current schedules and budgets against the original plan.

84 Never relax control, even when all is going to plan.

85 Ask the team for ideas on speeding up progress.

MONITORING EFFECTIVELY

Keeping control of a project involves carefully managing your plan to keep it moving forward smoothly. Effective monitoring allows you to gather information so that you can measure and adjust progress toward the project's goals. It enables you to communicate project progress and changes to team members, stakeholders, superiors, and customers, and gives you the justification for making any necessary adjustments to the plan. It also enables you to measure current progress against that set out in the original plan.

MONITORING SUPPLIERS

External suppliers can be a threat, since you do not have direct control over their resources. Remember to ensure that you monitor their progress, too. Make them feel part of the team by inviting them to meetings and informal gatherings. This will help you to track their progress throughout their involvement in the project, rather than only when they are due to deliver.

UNDERSTANDING THE MONITORING PROCESS

Team members prepare progress reports

Project manager summarizes for sponsor and stakeholders

Items for discussion are listed on regular review meeting agenda

Regular review meeting is held to resolve issues and assess progress

Periodic meetings are held to monitor milestones

Plans are updated if necessary to keep project on track

USING REPORTS

Anyone responsible for an activity or a milestone must report on progress. Encourage the team to take reports seriously, and to submit them on time. Reports should record the current state of the project, achievements since the last report, and potential problems, opportunities, or threats to milestones. As project manager, you review the reports and summarize the current position for your sponsor and stakeholders. Having gauged the importance of issues reported, use a red, amber, and green status system to help you draw up your review meeting agenda, so that the most urgent items, or those with red status, take priority.

POINTS TO REMEMBER

- If the project is a large or complex one, reports will be required more frequently.

- When a project involves tackling issues for the first time, tight and frequent controls should be established.

- If team members are used to working on their own, too frequent monitoring may be counterproductive.

CONSIDERING TIMING

Think about how often you will need progress reports and review meetings. You may require weekly or even daily reports, depending on the potential harm a problem could do to the project were it not detected and reported. Regular review meetings provide an opportunity to resolve issues, discuss progress, and review performance. You should hold reviews at least once a month, and probably more often on a complex project, or a project going through a very demanding phase.

HOLDING REVIEW MEETINGS

Review meetings are held throughout the life of a project to discuss progress and achievements and mark milestones. Run these meetings effectively to encourage teamwork and provide all involved with an accurate picture of how the project is faring.

86 Encourage team members to speak out on any aspect of the project.

87 Ensure that review meetings are not tediously long.

88 If progress has been made, praise people's efforts.

PLANNING A REVIEW

There are two types of review meeting. A regular formal review occurs at least monthly to monitor detailed achievements and issues in implementing the plan. An event-driven review, to which stakeholders, such as your sponsor, will be invited is held as certain milestones are arrived at. These meetings are concerned with the business objectives of the project. They may be called to check that the project is meeting certain criteria. It is sometimes true that if the criteria are not met, the future of the project will be in doubt.

SELECTING ATTENDEES

You will need your sponsor at some meetings, but probably not all. Key team members will almost certainly attend all reviews, while other members should attend only if there is a valid reason for their attendance, or their time will be wasted. If someone need only be present for one or two items, estimate when you will reach those items and ask them to arrive a few minutes earlier. If you need to make a decision, ensure that the person with the authority to make the decision is present and that all the necessary information is available.

QUESTIONS TO ASK YOURSELF

Q Will every attendee have a valid contribution to make?

Q Are there some team members who only need to attend part of the meeting?

Q Is this team member attending the meeting because they have always done so, rather than for a specific purpose?

Q Does the absence of anyone pose a threat to the project?

Use progress report to compile agenda	→	Decide who needs to attend review	→	Circulate agenda to participants

CHAIRING A REVIEW

The key to chairing a review meeting successfully is good discipline. Summarize the objectives at the outset and allocate time to each item on the agenda. Focus the team on appraisal rather than analysis, using questions such as, "How is the project going?" and "What new issues have arisen since the last meeting?" Your aim is to keep everyone up to date with progress and give them a shared understanding of what is happening.

▲ PREPARING FOR MEETINGS
Key decisions are made at review meetings, so it is essential to prepare for them well. Send out agendas in advance to give the team time to do preparation work, too.

Team member arrives late for meeting

Project manager sets standards for punctuality in future

ESTABLISHING ▶ DISCIPLINE
Be prepared to be tough on latecomers. Make it clear from the outset that such behavior is unacceptable, stressing the fact that one person's lateness wastes everyone's time.

89 Remind people of the agenda when they stray from it.

90 Always seek to end a meeting on a positive note.

REINFORCING OBJECTIVES

Ensure that you return to the objectives throughout the meeting, recording which have been achieved, which remain, and how the meeting is going against the time plan. If people are straying from the point or talking irrelevantly, bring the discussion back to the main issue by saying, for example, "We are not here to discuss that today – let's get back to the point." At appropriate moments, summarize the views and decisions made. As objectives are achieved, consider releasing those people who are no longer needed.

OVERCOMING PROBLEMS

However sound the project plan, once you start to operate in the real world, problems will occur. Encourage team members to raise concerns, and use the discipne of problem-solving techniques to tackle difficulties as they arise.

91 Look at every aspect of a problem before trying to resolve it.

92 Remember that forewarned is forearmed.

93 Ask team members to bring you solutions as well as problems.

RAISING CONCERNS

Your primary aim is to identify problems early enough to prevent their becoming crises. It is far more difficult to take action when a problem has become urgent. Although you may create extra work by examining problems that do not ultimately occur, it is better to err on the side of caution than to find that a problem has escalated without your knowledge. With experience, the team will get better at judging whether and when to raise a concern. You should be particularly concerned to see that problems with a high impact on the project are spotted and action taken before they become high urgency as well.

◀ **HANDLING TENSIONS**

Since projects tend to be carried out alongside regular business operations, problems often result when the two are ongoing. In this case, the project members were trying to make improvements by identifying late deliveries. But by raising concerns too early, they were disrupting the usual warehouse work. By agreeing when to raise concerns, both teams were able to do their jobs more effectively.

CASE STUDY

John was put in charge of a new project to improve the inventory control system in his organization's main warehouse. However, once the project was under way, he was approached by Tom, the warehouse manager, who told John that he and his warehouse staff were having to spend an inordinate amount of time chasing up deliveries deemed to be late by a member of the project team. Tom explained that most of the queries raised by the team member were unnecessary, because the goods were generally delivered only a few hours late, and so asking warehouse staff to chase them seemed pointless. John called Tom and the project team together to agree when a query really needed to be raised. This reduced the strain on warehouse staff, and gave everyone more time to chase up deliveries that really were late.

DEALING WITH PROBLEMS

> **Listen to concerns raised by team members**

> **Discuss their impact and, if significant, look at the options with the team**

> **Take an overview and make a final decision**

> **Update the plan if the decision involves altering course**

> **Send updated plan to knowledge coordinator**

RESOLVING DIFFICULTIES

A useful problem-solving technique is to home in on four areas to find out which is causing difficulty. For example, if production is falling short of target, consider which of the following four P's could be the culprit:

● **People** Is the problem occurring because people do not have the right skills or support?
● **Product** Is there something wrong in the design of the product or the production method?
● **Process** Would an improvement in one of your business processes cure the problem?
● **Procurement** Is it something to do with the products and services we buy?

DO'S AND DON'TS

✔ Do keep in constant touch with suppliers who may be causing you problems.

✔ Do correct a recurring problem by changing a process.

✘ Don't start to resolve an issue until you have understood the whole problem.

✘ Don't assume that team members have problem-solving skills

UPDATING THE PLAN

Ask your project coordinator to document ongoing problem-solving activities in the knowledge center as open items, and assess them at your regular review meetings. Major issues may result in the need to make significant changes to the plan. It is even possible that new information or a change in the external environment will invalidate the project as it stands. Suppose, for example, that a competitor brings out a new product using components that makes your project irrelevant. This would be unfortunate, but since your priority is to deliver value to your organization, the best value may lie in scrapping the project.

94 Keep stakeholders informed if you change the plan.

95 Identify the cause of a problem to prevent it from happening again.

DEALING WITH CHANGE

Change is inevitable on projects, so flexibility is vital. Whether customers revise a brief or senior managers alter the scope of a project, you must be able to negotiate changes, adapt the plan, and keep everyone informed about what is happening.

96 Look at alternatives before changing a major component of the plan.

97 Explain the benefits of change to those affected by it.

98 Seek approval for any changes as quickly as possible.

UNDERSTANDING CHANGE

Some changes will be within your control, such as shortening the schedule because you and your team are learning how to complete activities more quickly as you work through the plan. Other changes will be imposed upon you, such as when a customer asks for something different, or a superior decides to poach two of your key team members to do another job. Alternatively, your monitoring system may have highlighted the need for a change to avoid a potential problem or threat. Whenever the need for change arises, it is vital to be able to adjust the project plan as necessary. You must also be able to measure whether the desired effect on the project has been achieved, so that you will know if the change has been successful.

◀ **DISCUSSING CHANGE**
Bring the team together to evaluate how changes might affect the project plan, looking at the proposed alterations against your original goals, order of activities, budget, people, resources, and time.

ASSESSING IMPACT

Before you commit to making any changes, assess their impact on the project. Ask the team to review how they will affect the schedule, budget, and resources. Examine the alternatives: is there another way to accomplish the project's objectives? If changes have to be made for the project to move forward, document them on the original plan, and gain approval from superiors, sponsors, and stakeholders before implementing them.

TACKLING CHANGE EFFECTIVELY

Discuss impact of change with the team

⬇

If change has a major impact, look at the alternatives

⬇

Document necessary changes on original plan

⬇

Seek approval from stakeholders and superiors

⬇

Inform everyone on the project of changes as soon as possible

RESISTING UNNECESSARY OR DETRIMENTAL CHANGES

When change is dictated, perhaps by a superior or sponsor, it may not always make sense. Determine whether carrying out the change will affect the eventual outcome of the project. If the change seems to be frivolous, or will have a negative impact on the project, make those imposing it aware of the benefits that will be lost. Be prepared to fight your corner, or to offer alternative solutions that will ensure your project still meets its objectives.

THINGS TO DO

1. Talk to the team about how changes will affect them.
2. Explain the rationale behind the changes and why they had to happen.
3. Redefine new objectives, time frames, or roles.
4. Discuss issues individually if anyone is still unhappy about the changes.

COMMUNICATING CHANGE

If your team has been working hard to achieve one set of objectives and is suddenly told that the goal posts have changed, people will inevitably feel demotivated. Talk to the team about change as soon as possible, particularly if roles are affected. Focus on the positive aspects of change, and be frank about why it is happening. Take people's concerns seriously, listen to their ideas, but stress the need to adapt as quickly as possible. Finally, spell out clearly any new expectations, schedules, or objectives in writing, so that everyone understands what should happen next.

MAXIMIZING IMPACT

As a project draws to a close, it is important to evaluate exactly what has been achieved and what can be learned for the next time. Take your project through a formal closure process that ties up all loose ends and marks its success.

99 Evaluate this project well to better manage the next one.

Q Is the sponsor satisfied that the original aims and business objectives of the project have been met?

Q Is the customer satisfied that he or she is receiving an improved service?

Q Have we spoken to all our stakeholders about final results?

Q Have I thanked all the contributors to the project?

Q Have all new insights and ideas been recorded?

SEEING PROJECTS THROUGH

Inevitably toward the end of a project, some team members will start to move to new assignments. It is important to keep remaining team members focused on final objectives until the very end of the project, when you write a formal closure report and hold a final meeting. You may have to protect your resources from being moved off the project too early, particularly if you want to avoid an untidy ending where the benefits are dissipated because final activities are completed haphazardly. Finally, you want your organization to learn as much as possible from the exercise and to ensure that the results you predicted are delivered in full.

LEARNING FROM PROJECTS

Talk to your knowledge coordinator about publishing a report explaining what the project achieved, and detailing relevant information such as facts gathered and processes used. If the project is likely to be repeated, meet with team members to go through the project from start to finish. Ask people to point out where, with hindsight, they could have made improvements. Your organization may benefit significantly if you produce a template for such a project plan, including an outline network and Gantt chart.

100 Ensure that you have not left any jobs unfinished.

101 Publicize the achievements of the project team.

COMPILING A CLOSURE REPORT

PARTS OF REPORT	FACTORS TO CONSIDER
PERFORMANCE INDICATORS A comparison of what the project has achieved against the original targets set.	● Explain in full the reasons for any variances between targets and actual achievements. ● Word the comparison in a way that validates the original investment appraisal.
RESOURCE UTILIZATION An assessment of the resources planned and those that were actually used.	● If the project used more or fewer resources than expected, state the reasons why. ● Include any information that will validate the budget allocated to the project.
STRENGTHS AND WEAKNESSES An appraisal of what went well on the project and what went wrong, or caused problems.	● Ask team members for input in order to conduct as thorough an analysis as possible. ● Make sure that the information recorded enables others to learn from this experience.
SUCCESS FACTORS A record of the top 10 factors judged as critical to the success of your project	● List your success factors with the help of the team, sponsor, and stakeholders. ● Create a list that will provide focus for future project managers.

THANKING THE TEAM

▼ **CELEBRATING SUCCESS**

Mark the end of a project with a celebration in recognition of the team's hard work and effort. This allows people to say their farewells and realize their achievements in a convivial atmosphere.

It is important that all the members of the team go their separate ways feeling as positive as possible, especially since you may want to work with the same people on subsequent projects. Indeed, good relationships should be kept up with all the stakeholders. Talk to everyone individually to thank them for their contributions. Hold a final meeting at which your sponsor can confirm that the project has indeed brought benefits and thank the team for its efforts. Your customers, in particular, may welcome an opportunity to express how they have found the results of the project.

ASSESSING YOUR PROJECT MANAGEMENT SKILLS

Evaluate your ability to think strategically by responding to the following statements, marking the option closest to your experience. Be as honest as you can: if your answer is "never," circle Option 1; if it is "always," circle Option 4, and so on. Add your scores together, and refer to the Analysis to see how well you scored. Use your answers to identify the areas that most need improvement.

OPTIONS
1 Never
2 Occasionally
3 Frequently
4 Always

1 I check whether I should treat a series of actions as a project.

| 1 | 2 | 3 | 4 |

2 I set specific, measurable objectives for projects.

| 1 | 2 | 3 | 4 |

3 I take time to plan a project thoroughly before starting work.

| 1 | 2 | 3 | 4 |

4 I fully understand the difficulties I face in achieving a project's objectives.

| 1 | 2 | 3 | 4 |

5 I have identified which of my project's resources are occupied on other projects.

| 1 | 2 | 3 | 4 |

6 I keep in regular contact with all stakeholders involved in my projects.

| 1 | 2 | 3 | 4 |

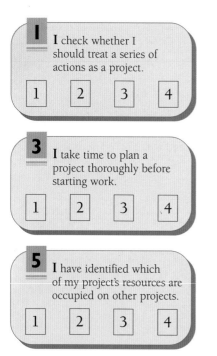

7 I always consider what the ideal outcome of a project would be.

1 2 3 4

8 I ensure that everyone clearly understands the project's objectives.

1 2 3 4

9 I set business targets for each part of a project.

1 2 3 4

10 I check that a project will not unnecessarily change what already works.

1 2 3 4

11 I compile a full list of project activities before I place them in correct order.

1 2 3 4

12 I calculate manpower time and elapsed time of all project activities.

1 2 3 4

13 I make sure all the key people have approved the plan before I start a project.

1 2 3 4

14 I liaise with the finance department to check the costs of a project.

1 2 3 4

15 I generally start project implementation with a pilot.

1 2 3 4

16 I keep a network diagram up to date throughout a project.

1 2 3 4

17 I inform all interested parties of changes to project resource requirements.

1   2   3   4

18 I prepare contingency plans for all major risks to the project.

1   2   3   4

19 I adapt my leadership style to suit circumstances and individuals.

1   2   3   4

20 I consider how best to develop my teams' skills.

1   2   3   4

21 I consider how well new team members will fit in with the rest of the team.

1   2   3   4

22 I make sure each team member knows exactly what is expected of them.

1   2   3   4

23 I use my sponsor to help motivate my team.

1   2   3   4

24 I have documented and circulated the primary milestones of the project.

1   2   3   4

25 I ensure that every team member has access to the information they need.

1   2   3   4

26 I avoid keeping secrets from the project team and stakeholders.

1   2   3   4

27 I ask people to attend review meetings only if they really need to be present.

| 1 | 2 | 3 | 4 |

28 I use the same standard method of reporting progress to all stakeholders.

| 1 | 2 | 3 | 4 |

29 I prepare the objectives and agenda of meetings.

| 1 | 2 | 3 | 4 |

30 I use a logical process to make decisions with my project team.

| 1 | 2 | 3 | 4 |

31 I keep my sponsor fully up to date with progress on the project plan.

| 1 | 2 | 3 | 4 |

32 I use problem-solving techniques to arrive at decisions.

| 1 | 2 | 3 | 4 |

ANALYSIS

Now you have completed the self-assessment, add up your total score and check your performance by referring to the corresponding evaluation below. Whatever level of success you have achieved, there is always room for improvement. Identify your weakest areas and refer to the relevant sections to refine your skills.

32–64: You are not yet sufficiently well-organized to ensure that a complex project will achieve its objectives. Review the planning process thoroughly and make sure that you follow it through step-by-step.

65–95: You are a reasonably effective project manager, but need to address some weak points.

96–128: You are an excellent project manager. Be careful not to become complacent or to let your high standards slip.

INDEX

A

absolute costing, 29
activities:
  agreeing dates, 34–35
  information management, 52
  listing activities, 24–27
  ordering activities, 32–33
  start-up phase, 26
aims *see* objectives
analytical leadership style, 44
Australia, cultural differences, 8

B

brainstorming:
  decision-making, 50
  listing activities, 25
  potential threats, 36
budgets:
  estimating costs, 29
  estimating manpower, 28

C

chairing review meetings, 59
change:
  dealing with, 62–63
  limits to, 22
charts:
  Gantt charts, 34–35
  holiday commitments, 35
closure stage, 7
  activities, 26
  reports, 64–65
coordinators:
  information management, 53, 54
  key team role, 41
commitment:
  from team members, 10
  leadership styles, 46
commitment matrix:
  agreeing dates, 35
  building a team, 40
  documenting resources, 30
communication, 26
  dealing with change, 63
  emails, 54
  project plan, 11
  sharing knowledge, 54–55

  see also meetings; reports
compromises, 30
conflicts, resolving, 46
consensus decisions, 45
constraints, assessing, 22–23
contingency planning, 37
cost-benefit analysis, 31
costing methods, 29
criteria, for decision-making, 50–51
critic, key team role, 41
critical path, network diagrams, 33
customers:
  key team role, 9
  vision statement, 18

D

data *see* information
dates, agreeing, 34–35
decision-making, 50–51
  leadership styles, 44–47
defining projects, 6–7
democratic leadership style, 44
dictatorial leadership style, 44, 46
documenting resources, 30
driving forces, 14, 15

E

emails, 54
expert advice, 15
external contact, key team role, 41

F

feasibility, checking, 14–15
feedback, communication, 55
finances *see* budgets
flexibility, 11
forcefield analysis, 15

G

Gantt charts, 34–35
goals, 7, 10
grouping activities, 24, 26

I

ideas person, key team role, 41
implementer, key team role, 41
implementing a plan, 12, 38–55
  building a team, 40–41
  communication, 54–55

  decision-making, 50–51
  developing teamwork, 48–49
  effective leadership, 44–47
  information management, 52–53
  launching project, 42–43
  project manager's role, 38–39
  start-up reports, 43
indicators, setting objectives, 20
industry standards, 20
information:
  communication, 54–55
  management of, 52–53
  problem-solving, 61
  tracking progress, 56
initiation sessions, 42
inspector, key team role, 41
investment appraisal, 31

J

Japan, cultural differences, 45, 48

K

key project features, 7
key team roles, 8–9, 41
knowledge coordinator, 53, 54

L

launching projects, 42–43
leadership:
  developing teamwork, 48–49
  project manager's role, 38–39
  styles of, 44–47
listing activities, 24–27
logic, decision-making, 50

M

manpower, estimating needs, 28
marginal costing, 29
master schedule, 17
  agreeing dates, 35
meetings:
  final meetings, 64, 65
  initiation sessions, 42
  milestones, 32, 58
  problem-solving, 61
  review meetings, 57, 58–59
milestones:
  monitoring performance, 57

review meetings, 32, 58
start-up reports, 43
monitoring performance, 13, 56–65
  dealing with change, 62–63
  maximizing impact, 64–65
  overcoming problems, 60–61
  review meetings, 57, 58–59
  tracking progress, 56–57

N

network diagrams, 33
  agreeing dates, 34
North America *see* United States

O

objectives:
  review meetings, 59
  setting, 20–21
  vision statement, 18–19
opportunities, start-up reports, 43
ordering activities, 32–33
outside resources, 31

P

performance *see* monitoring performance
personality clashes, 46
pilot programs, 27
planning, 11, 18–37
  agreeing dates, 34–35
  assessing constraints, 22–23
  committing resources, 28–31
  defining the vision, 18–19
  listing activities, 24–27
  ordering activities, 32–33
  setting objectives, 20–21
  updating the plan, 61
  validating the plan, 36–37
  vision statement, 12
predicting success, 15
presentations, 26
prioritization, 16–17
  objectives, 21
  scheduling projects, 17
problems:
  identifying threats, 36
  overcoming, 60–61
  preempting, 37
progress reports, 26, 57

Q

quotes, outside resources, 31

R

reports:
  closure reports, 64–65
  progress reports, 26, 57
  start-up reports, 43
resisting forces, 15
resources, 7
  capitalizing on investments, 23
  committing, 28–31
  compromises, 30
  documenting, 30
  estimating costs, 29
  estimating manpower, 28
  limitations, 23
  outside resources, 31
  planning, 11
  prioritizing projects, 16
  scheduling projects, 17
review meetings, 57, 58–59
risks, start-up reports, 43
roles:
  key team roles, 8–9, 41
  project manager, 38–39

S

SAFE decision-making, 51
scheduling projects:
  estimating activity times, 32
  listing activities, 24
  master schedule, 17
sign-off, 31
sponsors:
  cultural differences, 8
  review meetings, 58
  role of, 8, 9
stages of project, 12–13
stakeholders:
  commitment matrix, 30
  communication with, 54, 55
  involvement of, 8
  listing activities, 25
  role of, 8, 9
  start-up reports, 43
  validating the plan, 36, 37
  vision, 12
standards, researching, 20
start-up stage, 26
  key feature of project, 7
  reports, 43
success:
  celebrating, 65
  predicting, 15
suppliers:
  monitoring, 57
  key role, 9
  quotes from, 31

T

targets:
  problem-solving, 61
  setting objectives, 21
  start-up reports, 43
teams:
  building, 40–41
  closing down, 64–65
  communication, 54–55
  dealing with change, 62–63
  decision-making, 50–51
  developing teamwork, 48–49
  estimating manpower needs, 28
  information management, 52–53
  key feature of project, 7
  key roles, 8–9, 41
  launching project, 42–43
  leadership styles, 44–47
  life stages, 48, 49
  resolving conflicts, 46
  review meetings, 58
  vacation commitments, 35
threats, identifying, 36
time:
  agreeing dates, 34–35
  assessing constraints, 22
  estimating activity times, 32
  feasibility, 14
  leadership styles, 46
  network diagrams, 33
  scheduling projects, 17
trials, 27

U

United States, cultural differences, 8, 45, 48, 53

V

vacation commitments, 35
validating the plan, 36–37
vision:
  defining, 18–19
  planning project, 12, 20
  start-up reports, 43

W

"window of opportunity", 22

ACKNOWLEDGMENTS

AUTHORS' ACKNOWLEDGMENTS

There was an impressive team of skilled people involved in producing this book. In particular we would like to thank Adèle Hayward and Caroline Marklew of Dorling Kindersley for their help in sorting out the concepts, structure, and overall design of the book. Arthur Brown brought constructive and creative ideas to the detailed design stage, and Amanda Lebentz is the most positive and meticulous editor you could hope to have. We gratefully acknowledge their huge contributions.

PUBLISHER'S ACKNOWLEDGMENTS

Dorling Kindersley would like to thank the following for their help and participation in producing this book:

Photography Steve Gorton.

Models Roger Andre, Angela Cameron, Anne Chapman, Sander deGroot, Emma Harris, Lucy Kelly, Peter Taylor, Roberta Woodhouse.

Make-up Janice Tee.

Picture research Andy Sansom.
Picture library assistance Melanie Simmonds.

Indexer Hilary Bird.

PICTURE CREDITS

Key: *a* above, *b* bottom, *c* centre, *l* left, *r* right, *t* top
Powerstock Photolibrary/Zefa 27, 31 *tr*; Index 51 *br*, 62 *bl*; Raoul Minsart 4; **Rex Interstock** Melanie/FOTEX front jacket; **Telegraph Colour Library** FPG/M Malyszko 64 *bl*; Ryanstock 19.

AUTHORS' BIOGRAPHIES

Andy Bruce is the founder of SofTools Limited – a specialist business research and consulting company. Following completion of a largely academic MBA programme, he has spent the past eight years helping a variety of organizations manage major projects and cope with change in the real world – more information on tools and techniques can be found at www.SofTools.net.

Ken Langdon has a background in sales and marketing in the computer industry. During his early years with a major computer supplier, he was involved in pioneering the use of project management techniques – including a comprehensive use of Pert – in the information technology departments of major computer users in industry and local government. As a consultant he has taught project planning techniques and assisted in the preparation of plans in the USA, Europe and Australasia.